Stay Organized While You Study

TRIGGER™

The mental health & wellbeing publisher

Stay Organized While You Study
BY LAUREN CALLAGHAN

Lauren Callaghan (CPsychol, AFBPsS, PGDipClinPsych, PgCert, MA (hons), LLB (hons), BA) is a highly regarded clinical psychologist. She has worked at world-renowned research centres in London, UK, where she was recognised as a leading psychologist in the field of anxiety problems including obsessional and perfectionism problems. Lauren received further qualifications in systemic family therapy and uses her expert skill set to work with individuals and their families to overcome their mental health difficulties. During her years of clinical practice, Lauren has worked with a number of students suffering from anxiety, poor time management and perfectionism, and wants to help students to improve their mental health and wellbeing. After running a successful practice in London, she has recently moved to Sydney, where she continues to work as a clinical psychologist.

Stay Organized While You Study

Make the Most of your Student Experience

LAUREN CALLAGHAN

TRIGGER
The mental health & wellbeing publisher

First published in 2020
This edition published in 2023 by Trigger Publishing
An imprint of Shaw Callaghan Ltd

UK Office
The Stanley Building
7 Pancras Square
Kings Cross
London N1C 4AG

US Office
On Point Executive Center, Inc
3030 N Rocky Point Drive W
Suite 150
Tampa, FL 33607
www.triggerhub.org

A CIP catalogue record for this book is available
upon request from the British Library
ISBN: 9781837963775
Ebook ISBN: 9781837963782

Cover design by stevewilliamscreative.com
Typeset by Fusion Graphic Design

*To all hard working, sleep deprived,
time-challenged students.*

ROLE DEFINITIONS

A Who's Who of Student Support

Doctor (general practitioner)

A medically qualified doctor who sees people in the community, not in a hospital, and is able to help with all conditions, although they may have a special interest, for example in skin problems or mental health. They are sometimes called a "family doctor", and will often refer to specialists, such as psychiatrists or psychologists, for specific problems.

Counselor

A counselor offers a safe, confidential space for individuals to talk. Counselors help their clients explore their thoughts, feelings and actions to help them come to terms with life and find more hopeful and useful ways to approach their future. Counselors will work in different ways, depending on their training, but will always allow their client to take the lead in what they want to talk about. They do not offer advice, but through the empathic attention they give to their client's words, the client often discovers their own wisdom, helping them to lead a more fulfilling life.

Clinical Psychologist

A person who specializes in psychological or emotional conditions, and mental health disorders. They will have specialized in the study of clinical psychology and will usually have a doctorate or PhD (though they're not medically qualified, and will not able to prescribe medication). They assess people and diagnose mental health conditions or problems. They are trained in using talking and behavioral interventions specifically tailored to treat psychological disorders. They may use a range of therapy approaches, which vary from psychodynamic to cognitive behavioral therapy, family and couples' therapies to interpersonal approaches. They base their assessment and treatment methods on scientific principles and outcomes and will use the best evidenced method that helps to treat an individual.

Therapist
A term for professionals who use talking and behavioral therapies to support people with mental health conditions.

Psychiatrist
A medically qualified doctor who specializes in mental health conditions – also called psychiatric conditions – who can assess, make a diagnosis, offer advice, and prescribe medications. A psychiatrist is the only person who can prescribe specialist medications. They work with doctors, therapists, psychologists and counselors and will usually recommend a type of talking or behavioral treatment.

CONTENTS

INTRODUCTION

Starting college or university is a big deal – it is likely to be the first time you are fully on your own, living away from home, independent and answerable to yourself for your own behavior. This also means you are responsible for managing your time, organizing yourself to meet deadlines, study and pass exams, and finish research projects, as well as taking care of all the other life and university commitments – eating, sleeping, socializing, exercising, dating, laundry, cooking, cleaning, appointments, family obligations, hobbies, part-time work... That's a lot of stuff to fit in alongside your course (the reason you are there in the first place, remember!), which you likely have paid a lot of money to do.

Long gone are the days when going to university was seen as having time to party a lot and socialize. While these are important and fun things to do while you are there, many people are now competing for restricted places on undergraduate and graduate courses, and then competing for jobs in the workforce. Students work hard and work long hours, and many need to hold down part-time jobs to help finance their studies. Universities are offering summer, evening, online and condensed courses so people can get their degrees and enter the workforce sooner (and pay off that student loan sooner). So, university can be stressful and competitive, but at the same time it is an amazing adventure where you will learn new ideas and establish lifelong friendships. And consequently, it is important to be organized to make the most of your time there.

Why I Wrote This Book

I was once at university too – although it seems like a long time ago now. I would have found a book like this, giving me advice on how to organize myself, incredibly helpful. I discovered strategies for organizing myself that worked, and also those that didn't work, the hard way – by trial and error. Given I was at university a long time (completing graduate studies and then clinical psychology training) I managed to figure out over time what worked for me, and what didn't. But had I learnt these strategies sooner I would have saved a lot of time, slept more and felt less stressed. I have written this book in the hope that you won't have to spend years learning what helps you to be organized, and you can feel better prepared for university.

This book aims to help you:

- Be more aware of how you spend your time.
- Become more effective managing your time and consequently your studies.
- Develop better strategies for organizing yourself.
- Feel more on top of your coursework.
- Feel less stressed and anxious.
- Identify and solve problems with organizing yourself.
- Develop better self-management habits for life.

I sincerely hope you find this book useful. It was written with you in mind and based on real life experiences at university, working with students who had trouble managing themselves and the multiple demands of being at university. Remember, too, this book is a guide, and you may not choose to use all the strategies suggested. But please try different ones, and work out what works for you. I promise it will be worth it in the long run and make your time at university more enjoyable.

CHAPTER 1

WHY IT IS IMPORTANT TO BE ORGANIZED WHILE YOU STUDY

Research shows that college students who have good sense of time, and who know how they spend their time, do better academically. In fact, the ability to manage one's time, study effectively and strategically, is considered fundamental to success at university.

Ever said, 'I'm just a last-minute kind of person?', or 'I wish I could be more like them – the organized person who always has tabbed study notes?', or 'I wish I could stop procrastinating!' Well, the good news is that you can become more organized with your time and coursework, and consequently become a more organized student. Organizational skills can be learned! You can train yourself to be better with your time, and more organized. Not only this will mean you are more likely to achieve academic success, but these are skills that you can apply at any stage in life – when you leave university and start work, for example. Also, using your time better and learning to work more effectively means that you are less likely to panic around exam time and when projects are due, and feel less stressed and anxious overall.

The good news
Being in control of your time may not come naturally to
you but it is something that you can learn. There is no
secret formula. Good organization and time management
is based on psychology, behaviors and strategies.

The psychology behind it all

Psychologists love to try to understand human behavior.
We look at why people do the things they do, and why they
feel the way they feel. Basically, it comes down to how we
'think' about a situation or event. This then affects how we
'feel' emotionally, and what we do about it. This helps us to
pinpoint how to help people who might be feeling distressed
and are behaving in ways that are counterproductive to what
they want to achieve.

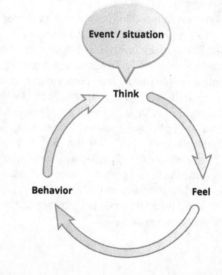

We can apply this type of analysis to how we organize ourselves and manage our time. The example below shows how we can organize and manage our time.

Jayne's Story

Jayne worries she has too much coursework to complete this term. She feels anxious and overwhelmed, and ends up procrastinating and not getting started on her work. This, in fact, makes her panic and she doesn't leave enough time to complete the work. Because she doesn't leave enough time to get her coursework done, she then feels even more worried and anxious. She feels paralyzed and doesn't know how to start her work or study, and this results in her handing in coursework late and being unprepared for exams.

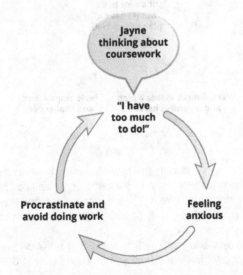

Jayne thinking about coursework

"I have too much to do!"

Procrastinate and avoid doing work

Feeling anxious

We call this a 'vicious cycle' – where the way we respond ends up keeping the problem going or making it worse.

Jayne's response of procrastinating and avoiding starting her work means that she continues to feel overwhelmed and anxious about her coursework. If she had been more organized and had some techniques in place to help her manage her time and reduce her anxiety, she would be able to complete her coursework on time and feel more prepared for exams. As a consequence, she would have felt less anxious overall. It would break the 'vicious cycle' she found herself caught up in.

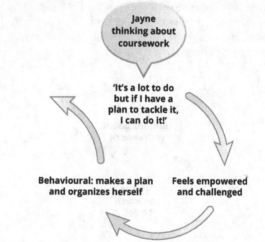

Jayne thinking about coursework

'It's a lot to do but if I have a plan to tackle it, I can do it!'

Behavioural: makes a plan and organizes herself

Feels empowered and challenged

This is just one example to show how your thoughts, feelings and responses link up and how being organized can help us. By changing her approach, Jayne managed to find a way out of the vicious cycle, stop procrastinating and complete her coursework on time.

Procrastination and feeling anxious at university are very common problems and they are discussed later in the book.

Good things come from being organized

Being organized and managing your time effectively at university will help you to create 'positive feedback loops', whereby your reaction to being organized is more successful studying, which further motivates you to continue your good time management in a kind of upward spiral. This makes good outcomes far more likely.

John's Story

John was in his second year of studying engineering. After a stressful start in his first year he decided to be more organized this year, and he put in place a number of strategies to help him feel more in control and complete his work on time. He made a good start in the first semester and found that not only was he feeling on top of his work, but he was getting higher grades, too. This led John to feel even more motivated to study and put more effort into his work.

As you can see with John, by changing his approach – his 'thinking' – he felt more motivated and engaged in his studies. This created a positive feedback loop, which resulted in him spending more time studying and on his coursework.

So you see, being organized and figuring out strategies to manage yourself and your time at university early on will have positive results. Not only will you feel less stressed, and more in control of your time and on top of your work, but you will hopefully see better grades too.

Good time management and self-organization

Knowing you are in control of time

Feels positive and motivated

Positive outcome with better grades

Summary

- Being organized at university will make you feel less stressed, and allow you to enjoy your time there more.
- The way you organize yourself is down to how you think about things, how you then feel and how you respond to these feelings.
- You can get caught up in 'vicious cycles' where your responses make you feel more overwhelmed and stressed, and make the problem worse.
- You can change the way you approach your time at university and your coursework, and create a way out of this vicious cycle.
- By changing your responses and approaches to organizing yourself, you can create positive feedback loops, which will mean you are more motivated and ready to study and complete coursework.

CHAPTER 2

KNOWING WHERE YOUR TIME GOES

One of the most common problems students have with organizing themselves at university is managing time, and this often starts with not having a thorough understanding of how you are using this precious resource in the first place. The good news is that you can learn some simple strategies to help address this. In this chapter, you will discover how to track your time for a week as a starting point to help you make better time decisions. You will see how underutilized time can be used more effectively, find out what your 'time suckers' are, and revamp your week to achieve more and hopefully feel less stressed about the things you need to do.

Help, I have no time!

Do you ever wonder how other people seem to get everything done in time, whereas you seem to struggle to get tasks completed? Do you get to Sunday night and think where did that week go? Do you always seem to be late to lectures and tutorials? Do you miss deadlines despite knowing about them for weeks and trying to be organized?

If so, it might be an issue of underestimating the amount of time things take, and not using your time effectively. The research suggests that students who have a good time perception are more successful academically. This means that students who know what they spend their time on are more likely to perform better and get better grades.

A simple but effective way to know where your time goes is to spend a week tracking your time. Doing this early on is also a great investment in your future at university, as you only need to do it once to know where your time goes, and then this knowledge enables you to use your time better from then on. Another benefit of tracking your time is to learn about where you might have space to fit in some more study, or perhaps some exercise or any other activity that you would like to do but are currently struggling to fit in.

How to track your time

The best way to track your time is by filling in a time sheet for the week. You can use a time sheet template online, or you might prefer to use one on your phone so you can sync it across your devices. See below for an example of a filled in sheet. When doing your own, I suggest you follow these guidelines:

- Divide each day into twenty-four one-hour blocks and account for *all* of your time in the week. Using one-hour blocks should be fine, and you can write more than one thing in each slot, as life doesn't really happen in one-hour blocks! For example, an hour block might incorporate 'breakfast, shower, pack bag, coffee, walk to uni'.
- Fill it in as you go along during your day: if you try to account for the whole day at 11 p.m. you will forget the nuances – you won't remember that you spent twenty minutes chatting to a fellow student about the essay after your lecture, or the fifteen minutes you spent scrolling through Instagram after lunch.
- It is good to be as detailed (and honest!) as possible in order to really learn where your time goes. For example, in Haley's week below she could have just written an 'hour' of study, but she added detail, recording: 'forty-five

minutes study, fifteen minutes playing game on phone'.
- It doesn't matter if at the end of the week you think you have tracked an 'abnormal' week. Every week will be different, and your studying, coursework and social events will change. The goal is to understand *how* you use your time, and hopefully find places where you can utilize spare time or time that is not being used effectively.
- BE HONEST! The only purpose of this exercise is to see where your time goes, and to help you make decisions for the future. It is for you to see – no one else – so you don't have to pretend you are studying when you are not, or that you are not scrolling the internet or playing on your phone. So, be truthful and detailed.

What to do with the results

Once you have tracked your time, you can analyze the data as a real scientist. See what trends you pick up, the items that surprise you and areas where you would like to improve. Then see if you can action some simple changes, such as those in the example below, to free up some extra time.

Haley analyzed the week that she tracked and made the following observations:

- She was pleasantly surprised that she was spending a good amount of time on coursework.
- She was disappointed that she was spending so much time on social media while she was studying – she thought that she was only using it every now and again as a break, and to relax before bed.
- Haley had wanted to exercise more, as she used to do a lot of sport at school, but could see that she was struggling to find the time to fit it in as much as she would like.
- Haley also thought she was spending too much time on food shopping, preparation and cooking meals. She likes

to eat healthily and didn't want to compromise the quality of her diet, but she wanted to make meal preparation quicker.

Here is a sample from her week:

	Monday	Tuesday	Wednesday
6	sleep	sleep	sleep
7	sleep	get up / shower / eat	get up / shower / eat
8	get up / shower / eat	study	go to uni
9	take bus to uni / play on phone	go to uni / walk	lecture
10	lecture	lecture	coffee / break with friend
11	lecture	stay after to talk to prof re topic / get coffee	library to research
12	chat to friends / eat lunch	lecture	library to research
13	go to student finance to make appointment	lab	read paper for lecture
14	tutorial	library to study / 15 min phone play	lecture
15	lecture	library to study / 15 min phone play	chat with friends
16	lecture / walk home	go to uni gym	head home
17	relax / play on phone	gym	watch Netflix
18	prepare food	walk home	prepare food
19	eat dinner	eat dinner	eat dinner
20	do some reading	talk to flatmate	play on phone
21	watch Netflx	watch Netlifx	online shopping
22	play on phone	do some internet research	online shopping
23	bed / sleep	bed / sleep	bed / sleep
24	sleep	sleep	sleep
1	sleep	sleep	sleep
2	sleep	sleep	sleep
3	sleep	sleep	sleep
4	sleep	sleep	sleep
5	sleep	sleep	sleep

She was then able to plan some improvements in her use of time:

- Haley definitely wanted to reduce her social media time. It wasn't a problem using it for a break, but she was using it too often, for too long. She decided to use it for five minute blocks as a break every twenty-five minutes while doing course work or study. She set an alarm on her phone for the twenty minutes study, which passed by quickly, and then again for five minutes free time to browse on her phone. Setting an alarm helped her keep to her timetable and she found that it motivated her to maximize her twenty minute study time in each twenty-five minute block.
- After tracking her time, Haley also saw that she had some spare pockets of time in the morning before heading off to university. She planned to try to fit in a twenty minute yoga or exercise video before breakfast a few times a week.
- Haley decided to plan her meals for the week on a Sunday so she knew what she needed to buy, and then to make large batches of food so she could freeze some meals, and sometimes take leftovers for lunch. She figured this would save her at least a couple of hours a week meal preparation time and would also save some money.

Watch out for time suckers

Time suckers are a pretty self-explanatory concept – things that seem to suck up your time, especially if left unchecked and unfenced. What I mean by unfenced is that there is not a natural end or finishing point, such as when you take a 'shopping excursion', which might start on a Saturday morning but then seems to last the whole day.

This does not mean that every non-academic activity is a time sucker – some activities, when used in moderation, can be a helpful and positive way to spend leisure time. But if they use up a lot of time, are not benefitting your goals (**see** p19) and it is hard to stop doing them, then they have probably turned into a time sucker.

Common time suckers include:

- Watching TV
- Spending time browsing at shops
- Surfing the internet
- Gaming
- Social media
- Hanging with your housemates
- Partying

Remember, these things are not necessarily bad in themselves, but they can take up too much time if you let them. Spending time with friends is important, as is socializing with the people you live with, but if you are finding yourself spending hours every night in the common space at the dorm talking to people you don't really know, and are not getting your coursework done, then that's not a great use of your time. Similarly, if you are spending up to an hour a day on your phone, messaging and scrolling through Instagram, it is probably fine. But if you spend three hours a day on Instagram and making TikTok videos, it's probably too much.

You may have a good idea about what your time suckers are already but, if you're not sure, have a look at your week after tracking your time, and they should become clear. Once you've identified them, the solution to overcoming your time suckers is usually fairly obvious and easy to implement. For example, you could set alarms on your phone like Haley, organize a study buddy to check in on you to make sure you are studying, or put your phone in a drawer while you are working. You can be creative too – you might put a 'Do Not Disturb' sign on your door to tell your flatmates that you are studying and prevent unwanted (but enjoyable) intrusions.

Look for underutilized time

Underutilized time is time that is misspent or not used effectively, and you will find this tucked away in places in your week where you might not have thought twice about it before. Everyone has underutilized time that they could use differently, and there are usually three reasons for this:

- We are not aware of the time.
- We think it is too insignificant a time period to use effectively.
- We are not organized about using it.

So, it is a matter of being aware of it, and then knowing what to do with it.

These pockets of underutilized time can be found once you have tracked your time for a week. They may also be apparent if you just spend some time thinking about when you often find yourself at a 'loose end' and spend time playing on your phone, or doing other mindless activities.

David's Story

David finishes his class at 3 p.m., and his girlfriend Sara finishes her tutorial at 3.45 p.m. in another campus building. David likes to wait and walk back to the halls of residence with Sara. He usually waits for her outside the tutorial and just plays on his phone. However, after tracking his time, he realized that this is a thirty-five minute window he could utilize better. He now finds a quiet place near Sara's tutorial to review his lecture notes for the day and start on his reading for the following week's class.

Amita's Story

Amita gets woken up by traffic noise outside where she lives, which starts to get loud around 7 a.m. Instead of lying in bed for half an hour, annoyed and trying to get back to sleep, she realized she could get up and use that time to pack her bag and organize herself for the day in a relaxed manner – collecting together any notes, readings and books she might need – instead of doing it last-minute and rushing out the door late to her first class!

You may know where your underutilized time lies just by thinking about it – for example, obvious periods include commuting or travel time, waiting in between classes or for meetings or appointments, or waiting to meet up with people.

Look at the week where you tracked your time and see if there are any identifiable spare blocks of time – even ten or fifteen minute blocks can be used differently. If you have five or six of these a day, that's over an hour of time that you could use in a better way.

Once you have identified periods of time that could be used differently, organize yourself so you are prepared to use this time when it comes up each week. You might ensure that you are carrying a textbook you can dip into, or spend the time reviewing notes or listening to lectures or lecture notes. Or you may choose to take the opportunity for some reflection or thinking time, or perhaps meditation or listening to music if that is something that you find relaxing. There are lots of beneficial ways to use these small pockets of time – you just have to prepare a little in advance and action your plans.

Summary

- A good way to see where you spend your time is to track it in detail for a week.
- This will help you be aware of your time and plan to use it more effectively.
- Track it daily in hour blocks and be honest with yourself.
- Look for underutilized time and note down any time suckers.
- Use this information to plan your time more effectively so you can harness even the smallest amounts of time for your benefit.

CHAPTER 3

TIME DEMANDS AND SETTING GOALS

This chapter looks at what further demands you have on your time – whether they are study-related demands or other things that require time, such as your personal relationships, paid or voluntary work, or just living. It aims to help you identify and set goals, so you can best manage your time to make the most of university.

Time management

Being organized while you study means developing routines or patterns of behavior so that you use your time effectively to manage the different demands on your life. You will find that while you are at university, there are plenty of things clamouring for your attention, not just your coursework. This pretty lengthy list includes:

- Studying for exams
- Coursework, group work, projects
- Thesis
- Socializing
- Dating
- Working part-time
- Family relationships
- Children (if you are a parent)
- Friendships
- Exercise

- Planning and cooking healthy meals
- Extra credit activities (research or tutoring)
- Volunteering
- Practising religion
- Physical health issues
- Mental health issues
- Hobbies and leisure activities

And sure, some of these things overlap, for example, you might go jogging with a friend for both social and health benefits, or you might work part-time in a bar for both financial and social reasons, or you might volunteer for extra credit and to spend time with your friends. But the trick is managing your time to fit in all those things that you want or have to do, and making it as stress free as possible.

Also, these demands may change during your time at university. You may take on some extra tasks to help with your course, or develop a significant relationship with someone. Or someone in your family might become unwell, or you might have some health issues. It can help to review your time demands regularly, to see what has changed so you can adjust your management of your time to cater for these new demands.

Effective time management is the ability to plan and control how you spend the hours in your day to accomplish your goals. For example, you might need to fit in research for your paper due next week, see your boyfriend or girlfriend, go to the gym and do a load of laundry that has been waiting for a few days. This will involve juggling time between the different areas and demands in your life.

Managing your time properly is perhaps the most important way of staying organized at university. It requires that you learn how to monitor your time so you can see how you actually spend it, cleverly using small pockets of free time and reducing the time spent on non-essential activities (as discussed in Chapter 2). But equally importantly, effective time management also requires that you establish clear goals and put them in order of priority, so that you set aside enough time to accomplish them.

Goals and values

Goals are specific, reachable ends that can be measured. These can be seen in terms of time, achievements or another specific measurement. For example, spending three hours on study, completing your degree or running 5km in your personal best time. The key requirements are that they are measurable and have an end date.

Setting goals is very important – it helps you have a plan for what you want to achieve. If you needed to go shopping to buy a present for a special occasion, you wouldn't just jump on a bus and hope that you end up somewhere where you can buy a gift. You would plan out who you need to buy it for, where you would most likely need to go, and what time would be best to make the trip. So, you would set some goals: to buy an appropriate present for the person, make a plan how to get it, and action the plan so it is ready in time for the special occasion. The same principle applies to university. You need to set goals, ascertain your timeframe and work out a strategy how to accomplish them. Your goals should be set for the short term, medium term and the long term.

Values are guidelines by which we live. Unlike goals, they are not measurable by a specific end date or number. Rather, they are guides that influence our behavior. They include morals, ethics and beliefs, and will have a strong impact on the way we act. For example, if you are passionate about environmental issues, you will likely live in a more sustainable manner and your choices – about what you eat, buy and how you live – will be guided by your environmental beliefs. I include values in this chapter as it is important when you are setting your goals to also consider your values. You are much more likely to achieve your goals if they are consistent with your values. If you believe that giving your time to good causes is as important as studying and getting your degree, you will organize your non-academic time to ensure that it prioritizes volunteering and charity work. If being in peak physical health is one of your values, you will ensure you make time for gym sessions over going to the student bar.

Take some time to think about the values that you live by, and note them down. It will be important to check in with these when you are setting goals to ensure they fit together well.

How much time do I need to achieve my goals?

Well, the best way to look at this is actually in reverse – how much time do you *have* to achieve your goals? The simple answer is: twenty-four hours a day or 168 hours a week. That is to say, you have the same amount of time as everybody else. It's not a question of how much time things require, it is an issue of how much time you want to devote to each goal. *You* get to decide how you spend your 168 hours.

Do you ever look at the star athlete who manages to train and compete, as well as maintain a straight A average, or that student who looks after their sick mother, holds down a part-time job and still manages to stay top of the class, and ask how do they fit it all in? It is no secret – we all have the same amount of time in a day. That star athlete might just be better at prioritizing their time and organizing themselves – they might be very disciplined and only spend one night a week socializing, and get up every morning at 6 a.m. to train. That top student has to go straight to her part-time work after class and work a six-hour shift so they don't spend forty minutes on Instagram, or three hours watching the latest drama on Netflix. These are not necessarily bad things to spend your time on – relaxing and connecting with others socially is important – but if you spend more time on these than study and work, then it might not be the best use of your twenty-four hours.

So, we all have 168 hours a week available. Take out fifty-six hours for sleep and you still have 112 hours to play with. You may argue that you need more sleep than the average person, but research has consistently shown that young adults need six to eight hours of sleep a day. So, unless you have a medical condition that requires more sleep, you are still working within the same time parameters as every other adult. Using our 112 waking hours wisely comes down to a case of what we prioritize and value, and spending our time on things that are important to us.

Working on your academic goals

Your goals will include both academic and non-academic aims. While your non-academic goals are also important, the main aim of this book is to help you to get and stay organized while you study, so I suggest separating out your academic goals for university first, prioritizing these ahead of your non-academic goals.

In order to work on your academic goals first spend some time looking at your course and its requirements. Courses will usually have a suggested time requirement, and will detail the assessment criteria. This will help you know what is expected and plan for it.

Now, write down your academic goals for the long term, medium term and short term of your time at university. Use the example on p27 (Junaid's case study) to help you do this. The trick is to try to break down your long-term goals into medium-term goals, and your medium-term goals into short-term goals. You will need to review your short-term goals regularly to ensure that you are making progress, and I suggest that you do this weekly. You'll also revise your whole list regularly, especially the short- and medium-term goals, as time passes and you achieve your goals and need to set new ones.

Goal	Time frame
Short-term	
Medium-term	
Long-term	

When you have written down your university goals, the next step is to assign your shorter-term goals a more detailed estimation of time. This will help you to plan your time each week and divide up your precious 168 hours.

Junaid's Story

Junaid was in his first year of a psychology degree and wanted to become a psychologist. It meant that he had to pass his undergraduate degree with first class honors, before applying for graduate school. His goals for his first year at university looked like this:

Long-term: Gain a first-class honors degree
Finish the first year with an A average
Apply for internships / summer jobs to help support the degree
Volunteer work
Seek out a mentor

Medium-term: Finish the research paper due at the end of the semester
Complete group project
Study and pass two exams

Short-term: Find a research topic for paper due end of semester
Make a plan with the group for the project
Revise two modules covered in lectures already

Junaid estimated that the time his short-term goals would take in the first week were as follows:

- Find a research topic for essay this week — 3–4 hours
- Make a plan with the group for the project — 2 hours
- Study 2 modules — 8 hours

You can see how Junaid broke down his longer-term goals into smaller chunks for his medium-term goals, and in smaller chunks again for his short-term goals. All goals can be broken down into smaller steps, and doing this will help to turn a big longer-term goal into manageable smaller ones.

Working on your non-academic goals

Now take a look at your values again – a lot of these will be non-academic. However, they are important to keep you well and give you purpose. Some of these values will translate into goals with specific ways you can measure them, whereas some of them might be more ethics or guidelines by which you live your life. For example, a value of being a good citizen in your community might translate into spending two hours volunteering at the local citizens' advice bureau each week.

Junaid's Story

Junaid's non-academic goals and values were to:

- Keep healthy and get fitter
- Spend time with girlfriend (she was at a different university so this included weekend trips and Facetime calls)
- Be more environmentally friendly (this was one of Junaid's values)
- Try some new activities

So, each week when setting time for his short-term goals, Junaid would also review this list and make time for these goals. For example, this week he planned to go for a twenty minute run three times a week, made some dates to speak with his girlfriend and planned to go see her at the end of the month. He also booked to go rock climbing at the student gym with a couple of friends from his dorm.

By reviewing his time demands, Junaid was able to plan in both academic and non-academic short-term goals for his week. Even if he didn't manage to achieve everything on his list (more on this in Chapter 4), by making a plan he was giving himself the best chance at achieving his short-term goals, and this helped prevent him from drifting through his week and finding he hadn't spent enough time on the things he really needed too.

The impact of achieving goals

The nice thing about achieving goals is that it creates an upward momentum – it makes us feel proud of ourselves, motivated to set more goals and more likely to put in the effort to achieve these goals. As you will recall from Chapter 1, when you change your approach, you can create a positive feedback loop in which more positive things happen, such as feeling less stressed, being more engaged in your studies and getting better results. Goals need to be challenging, but it is important that the goals you set yourself are also achievable, so you have every chance of meeting them. For example, setting a goal of studying for six hours straight without any breaks is pretty unrealistic, but studying for forty minutes out of every hour during a library session is more likely to be achieved. Recognizing this will make you more motivated to try to meet this goal, feeding into the likelihood of it being achieved and giving you the confidence boost to continue this upward spiral.

Summary

- There will be a lot of different demands on your time while you are university.
- It is good to know what these demands are likely to be so you can plan for them.
- You have 168 hours a week – around 112 hours awake – that you can use to meet your goals. You have enough time to do things – it is about how you use that time.
- Writing a list of your academic goals will keep you focused and allow for you to plan your time in order to meet your goals.
- Non-academic goals are also important, and you need to plan for these weekly after your academic goals.
- Start working on your short-term goals but remember to regularly review your medium- and long-term goals, too, to ensure they haven't changed, and that you remain on track to achieve them.

CHAPTER 4

HOW TO ORGANIZE YOUR TIME

This chapter will provide you with eight practical steps to help you effectively manage your time and achieve your study goals. Some of them might be things you have tried before with varying degrees of success, but please consider trying them again. Often things need a small tweak to work better – for example if you have tried a weekly timetable you may have used blocks of time that are too large or too small to be useful, or perhaps you didn't allocate enough time for the non-academic demands of living student life, or you may have set unrealistic study targets which made you feel less motivated to try to keep to your plan.

The eight steps are based on using a diary or calendar to help keep you focused on your goals. Online or paper diaries are both fine, but online diaries do have the benefit of being easier to amend and sync to all your devices.

1. Take it one week at a time

During each term or semester, it is best to take each week as a block of time – 168 hours – and then divide it into smaller chunks of time. Most planners or calendars divide up the day into hourly chunks, and some divide these further into thirty or even fifteen minute blocks. It depends on what you prefer, but for your purposes, hour blocks should be fine. Most online calendars are divided into hourly blocks but you can amend these time frames if needed. If you prefer a paper version so you can print it out and pin it on your wall, you can find these online for free.

	Mon	Tues	Wed	Thurs	Fri	Sat	Sun
7-8 a.m.							
8-9 a.m.							
9-10 a.m.							
10-11 a.m.							
11-12 p.m.							
12-1 p.m.							
1-2 p.m.							
2-3 p.m.							
3-4 p.m.							
4-5 p.m.							
5-6 p.m.							
6-7 p.m.							
7-8 p.m.							
8-9 p.m.							
9-10 p.m.							
10-11 p.m.							

2. Plan on a weekend, start on a Monday

It might seem logical to most people, but starting your weekly timetable on Monday is most sensible as this is when the university week starts. Allow for an hour on the weekend when you can sit and properly plan out your week – put an hour in your timetable each week to do this. Your weeks may be very similar – labs, lectures and tutorials won't change, and some of your extra curricular activities might stay the same, so you can copy regular events across rather than having to fill everything in from scratch each week.

3. Spend time on what is important to you

One of the most important elements of organizing your time effectively is knowing what is deserving of your time. You have had a look at where you spend your time in Chapter 2, and considered your goals and values in Chapter 3, and this will help you to judge what you deem deserving of your time and how much time to allocate to it.

Some things will be tasks with a clear beginning and end, such as writing an essay or going to tutorials. Some things won't be able to be measured by a clear ending but are still very important to you, such as spending time with friends or family, mentoring high school students, or coding a new app in your spare time. Even if they don't have the same clear ending, you can (and should) still apportion an amount of time to them. For example, you might diary for mentoring to take up two hours on a Tuesday, and you might want to allocate six hours of coding time your new app per week. Remember, however, to check your time demands and goals each week to ensure you are allocating enough time for your academic goals.

4. Essential vs. non-essential

It is also helpful to distinguish between essential items that will help you achieve your study goals, and non-essential items, perhaps with a simple colour-coding system. These non-essential items might still be very important to you, and add value to your life, but they are not directly related to your study goals. For example, exercise might be important to you and help you de-stress, but on its own it won't get that essay written. Playing Fortnite might help you connect with old friends from school, but on its own it won't help you pass your chemistry paper. If you label things like this as 'non-essential', when things don't quite go as planned – perhaps you are ill for a few days and get behind in your work – it will be easier for you to rearrange your upcoming timetable and take out some of the non-essentials when you can see clearly in your diary that you do have some chunks of time apportioned to such things that can be reapportioned in an emergency.

5. Prioritizing your time – diarize essential activities first

Once you have decided what is important to spend your time on, you need to prioritize these things to ensure that you spend time on them first. You might put study for exams as your first priority for the week, exercising as your second and spending time with friends as your third, for example.

Essential activities should be put in the diary first, and earlier in the week if possible. This is because if something ends up taking more time than expected – an essay may need a few extra hours on top of what you had planned, for example – you can move around your non-essential activities later in the week to make some time available.

6. Don't forget the basic living items

While it may not be as exciting or fun as hanging out with friends or learning about new philosophical theories in lectures, you still need to eat, sleep, wash and shower, clean your living space, buy groceries and toiletries, plan your finances, do laundry and other life admin tasks. So, don't forget to add these into your week when planning your time. You don't need to spell these out in minute detail – allowing an hour to get up, shower and have breakfast, do your dishes and leave for class can be consolidated into 'getting ready', for example. You might plan some down time in the evenings, but you don't have be overly descriptive.

7. Dedicate a realistic amount of time to each task or item

Once you have prioritized the things you want to spend time on this week, apportion them a sensible amount of time. Be careful not to underestimate the amount of time needed on a task or item, and remember to include extra time for things such as travel time, or going to the supermarket to get groceries, doctors appointments and calling your parents or grandmother. As you get practised at setting a timetable, you will realize which activities take longer than others. For example, giving yourself half an hour to travel to university according to the travel apps makes sense, but if after three weeks you work out that it usually takes you between forty-five minutes and an hour because the bus timings are inconsistent, then modify your future timetables accordingly.

8. Planning in advance and regularly reviewing your timetable

Each week, or 168 hours, will be different. There will be different demands on your time, different deadlines, different events and other things that come up. If you have a thesis due at the end of one semester, you will allocate more time for writing this in the last month of the term than the first month, for example. You can, however, save time by using a rough template for your weekly timetable, filling in as much information as you have at the beginning of the term or even academic year, and reviewing it regularly to fill in more detail.

This will help you to get a head start on your weekly planning sessions. You could fill it in as follows:

- Start with the permanent fixtures such as lectures, tutorials, study groups, labs and sports practices or gym classes, counseling sessions and part-time work.
- Then allocate time for general study, research or essays, and group or solo projects. You may not have the specific details when you put these hours in, but if you block them out in this way, each week you will find you have the time you need to catchup or complete your coursework, or study for exams.
- If you have a paper or coursework due, you can break down the general time set aside for study into more specifics: research, writing draft, review, edits, proofing and final read.
- Next add in the extra-curricular events that know about – for example, a birthday party, a special tutorial, a masterclass or extra lab, going for runs or to the gym, or social events.
- If you are working part-time and your hours change each week, ask for your shifts or rota in advance and fill in the weeks as far ahead as you can. This will allow you to plan your coursework demands alongside your employment.
- If you have any other booked fixtures in your term (or year) put diary these in advance. They might include gigs, plays, family events, weekends away, field trips, birthdays, etc. Having these in your diary in advance means you will spot them when you are reviewing your longer term timetable and planning your weeks and you can allow sufficient time for them and not be caught out by such events.

And remember you need to be flexible! A weekly timetable is a great way to help organize your time and feel less stressed. However, no matter how well you have planned out your time, life has a way of throwing us curveballs. There are always things that upset plans – illness (yours or someone you care for), relationship break-ups, mental health problems, physical health problems, emergencies, extra work shifts (you might really need the cash!), and many other interruptions. But the benefit of being organized and planning ahead is that you have the flexibility to absorb these things.

Summary

- Using a weekly timetable will help you organize your week effectively.
- Break it down into hourly chunks and put in essential items first, before allocating time to non-essential tasks.
- Organizing things in this way will give you the flexibility you might need if unexpected things happen.
- Be realistic with time, and modify your timings if things consistently take longer than you plan.

Save time by planning your diary in advance and review this regularly to be aware of what's coming up and to refine your timetable accordingly.

CHAPTER 5

BREAKS AND THINKING TIME

Planning for breaks in your study time or weekly timetable is crucial to academic success. You need breaks to recharge, and they help you stay motivated in your studies. Breaks are also important as they allow your brain absorb and process the information properly. This is also why sleep is important – our brains consolidate information and store it correctly while we rest, and this information can then be recalled at a later date. Think of it a bit like a computer coding new information to be stored on your hard-drive. Your brain is the computer, and you want to save some data and be able to bring it up later when you need it (i.e. in an exam or lecture). So you need to ensure the computer is inputting the data properly and saving it in the right place, in order for it to be recalled at will.

Breaks (including rest and sleep) will help your brain input and store this information correctly, to be recalled later. However, if you are too stressed, not studying effectively or too tired there can be problems with the inputting of data as well as the storing information. It might make it difficult to remember (recall) what you studied, or the idea might be corrupted and you can recall only part of it. In order to keep your brain working, it needs to regenerate and 'cool down' the engine, so to speak.

This chapter will discuss two types of break you might use – the micro break and the macro break – as well as looking at the benefits of allowing yourself some "thinking time" in your studies.

The micro break

This is the breather you need when you are studying or working. If you set a target of studying for six hours heading into exams, you'll realize you cannot possibly study for six hours straight. Whether or not you plan for a break, you will need one, so you end up finding ways to be distracted – maybe scrolling on your phone, checking Instagram, making coffee or filling your drink bottle, etc. This is not slacking, it is because you can't pay attention at full capacity for six hours straight. No one can! So, you might as well plan for a short break in your study time as you will be more likely to focus knowing you have a break coming up.

How long should I take a micro break for?

Everyone has a different work rhythm. Some would argue that in today's world we have a much more limited attention span than our ancestors, although I would argue that we are flooded with much more stimulus, too, and need to be able to sort through this quickly, which is what demands quicker shifts in attention.

The jury's out on the perfect study to break ratio, but there seems to be a general consensus that you need short 'micro' breaks frequently. The research suggests that you benefit from at least two short breaks of around five minutes every hour, and then a longer break of at least half an hour every two and a half to three hours.

But remember everyone is different – some people prefer a fifteen minute solid break every hour rather than a couple of shorter breaks in the hour. You also need to be realistic. If you think you can work for fifty minutes straight without a break – that means no checking your phone or emails, no chatting to others, no water or coffee breaks, just solid work – then try that. However, shorter breaks within the hour allow you time to get a drink, stretch and check those important text messages. You need to work out what's best for you.

The macro break

This refers to having longer periods of time away from study and coursework so you can really relax, enjoy life and come back motivated to hit the books again. It could be an evening out with friends, a day hiking, or even a weekend away exploring new places. It might be playing in a band or going to a sports tournament or film festival, or spending an evening practising yoga. It is important to have a complete break from study and coursework sometimes. This still has to fit in around your goals of completing your coursework and passing the year, so a weekend away right before exams might not be feasible, but going to the cinema one evening in the week before your exam to catch a film might be just what you need.

While there is no hard and fast rule on how many macro breaks is useful, you can work out what you need in order to stay effective and motivated to study. You may have a number of 'smaller' macro breaks in the week – maybe watching your favorite Netflix boxset or going to yoga every second day – and one or two 'larger' macro breaks, such as taking the afternoon off to go to the beach or for a hike, or catching up with friends for a sports match which takes most of the day. It is also important to have these breaks booked in your diary so you know you can plan for them, and this will also keep you motivated to achieve your study goals. It is much easier to complete a 10,000 word paper knowing you have a fun weekend planned when you finish it!

Distractions and thinking time

If you are working on projects and need new ideas or inspiration, breaks away from work can really help you have those lightbulb moments. Ever been stuck on a problem then, when you are in the middle of a completely different task, you come up with the answer? This is because sometimes changing environment and focus can allow our brains to shift gear and come up with the answer. There is research that backs up the idea that the brain is built to detect and respond to change, and shifting your attention to other things can enhance your performance on a task. It seems your brain needs a break from analytical thinking and will then come back at the task with renewed energy.

Also, having time to just 'think' or 'reflect' is important. Often, we get our best ideas in these moments. So, if you have to come up with research topics, or need some inspiration to finish an essay, it is definitely worth having some scheduled 'think' time away from your desk. It might be over a coffee, or walking in the park, but this thinking time is still 'work' and can be scheduled in on your weekly planner.

Summary

- It is important to plan for breaks in your study timetable so you can keep your brain working properly, and you come back to the tasks motivated and energized to learn.
- Micro breaks are the shorter breaks in each study period, and you need around two short breaks an hour.
- Macro breaks are longer periods of time away from coursework and study – they can be social or leisure activities and can include a weekend or evening away from study.
- Thinking time is also important, so make sure you allocate some time for this in your study plan.
- Breaking down tasks will make them more achievable and less overwhelming.

CHAPTER 6

HOW TO FIX SOME COMMON PROBLEMS

There are some common problems that people encounter when trying to organize themselves, but the good news is that there are lots of simple and practical things you can do to overcome them which will make a noticeable difference in your life.

Think about things differently

It can be easy to get caught up in a cycle of feeling stressed, then engaging in unhelpful responses to this, and thereby keeping the vicious cycle going. Remember Jayne (see p5) who felt overwhelmed by her amount of coursework, and thus avoided it by procrastinating, which made her feel even more stressed. Once she had figured out a new strategy to tackle her work, she was able to get on with doing it. She made a conscious decision to change her outlook to her work – which helped her to change her unhelpful responses. Instead of thinking, *'I have too much to do!'*, she changed her thinking to, *'It's a lot to do but if I have a plan to tackle it, I can do it'*. By changing her attitude, she is much more likely to stick to her new strategy. Sometimes, just by readjusting your outlook, you will overcome hurdles that are preventing you from being organized.

Here are some examples of common thinking problems that might get in the way of being organized with your coursework, and suggestions on how to reframe them.

Problematic thought	More helpful way of thinking
I have too much to do.	I have as much as anyone else to do, and I will make a plan to get it all done.
It will stress me out too much.	Anxiety is normal and if I have a plan in place, I will feel less stressed in the longer term.
I will do it later.	My reason to be at university is to pass my course and get my degree, so I will first do some work, and then go out for fun afterwards.
I don't have enough time.	I have the same amount of time as anyone else – and I can use my pockets of underutilized time better.
I don't know how to start.	If I just write my name, the title and a draft first sentence that is a good place to start.
I won't do a good enough job.	It doesn't have to be perfect; it has to be good enough to achieve my aims – a solid grade is enough.

Treat it like a job

When struggling with motivation for getting yourself organized while studying, it's worth remembering that university is designed to set you up for a job afterwards, whether it is working as an employee, being self-employed, creating your own business and so on. The important words here are 'working' and 'job'. Most of us need to earn money to finance our activities in life, and this is usually done by working at a job for some time in our life. In order to have job security and perform well, we turn up on time, and we work the hours required (often more!). It can be helpful to think of your time at university as a job – something that needs to take priority in terms of hours, where you are punctual and try your best to perform all tasks expected of you. This will help you make time to attend lectures, complete your coursework, and study for exams.

Your course will also give you an indication of how much time you can expect to spend attending lectures and tutorials, and on private study. For example, most people studying a full-time degree course will be expected to devote around thirty-five to forty hours a week to it.

Break it down

Have you ever looked at a task and thought, *'Where do I start!?'* The task may be large, overwhelming, complex, time-consuming or a combination of all of these things. One easy way to make tasks more manageable is to break them down. You can break down all tasks into easy manageable steps. Large projects, shorter essays, study time – whatever the end goal is – it can be broken down into smaller steps.

Deena's Story

Deena has a large research thesis (10,000 words) due at the end of the year. She is a bit stressed and doesn't really know how to start. With the help of her tutor she breaks down the task into steps:

1. Thinking about a research topic
2. Reading about the topic
3. Finalising her topic and checking the topic with her tutor

4. Finding some useful research papers on her topic
5. Coming up with five main ideas to put across in her paper
6. Planning out the research essay
7. Writing the paper

But even then, if it comes to writing the paper, she can break this down further – because the idea of just sitting down and writing 10,000 words is still pretty overwhelming! So, Deena comes up with a second plan and breaks the writing of the essay over the semester:

1. Write the introduction (250 words)
2. Then write one paragraph of approximately 500 words a night over eighteen nights
3. Write a summary conclusion paragraph of 500 words
4. Check references and add citations
5. Spell / grammar check and format
6. Final read through

Now her 10,000 word paper feels much more manageable, and she is looking forward to getting started on it! She can then put these goals into her weekly timetables over the semester so she works away at it steadily without getting stressed.

Organize your workspace and materials

Some students love having everything tabbed and organized according to size, color, shape and so on, whereas others write lecture notes on scraps of paper thrown into their bag never to be seen again. There is good evidence that students who are conscientious and well organized perform better academically – which is very logical as being organized with your work is a key study skill, and those with good study skills do well academically. But fear not if you don't consider yourself to be a naturally organized person – these are skills that can be learned! You can train yourself to be better organized, and organizing your materials bearing in mind the following tips is an easy place to start.

- Pack your bag the night before, or before breakfast to make sure you have everything you need for lectures and study for that day.
- Whether you are an old-school pen and paper note taker, or a computer or tablet user, make sure you have all the materials with you that you need to take notes – a charged laptop, stylus, paper, pens, etc.
- Put your notes in named files – whether binders, sleeves or electronic files – so you can retrieve them easily.
- If you miss a class, make sure you get the notes ASAP, read through them and add them to your files. It can be a nightmare trying to catch up on notes the week before exam time, especially if they are somebody else's notes as they will have their own form of shorthand that you might need help interpreting.
- Use your diary to record engagements and coursework and write in all your course readings and assignments as soon as you get them.

In addition to organizing your study materials, it's also important to organize your workspace. Most students will have a desk to work from, either at home or in their room. Having a dedicated workspace is very important – somewhere you can sit down and properly focus on work – and this doesn't mean your bed or the sofa or a beanbag.

You need to keep this space clear and ready for work at all times. If you have to shift layers of clothes, move makeup or food containers, empty cups and so on, it will not be an inviting place to sit down and focus.

Make sure you have good lighting to help you stay alert and focused. Natural light is best, but as you will often study in the evening or in winter when you won't have good access to natural light in your room, you will have to use a lamp or lights. It is suggested that a cool bright light (as opposed to a warm hue) mirroring daylight is the best for keeping alert and performing tasks that demand cognitive powers, such as studying.

Have a buddy (or two!)

It's a good idea to have a buddy system in place on your course, whereby if you are sick or unable to attend classes or tutorials for whatever reason, your buddy will collect handouts on your behalf and share their notes with you, and vice versa.

It can be useful to have a study buddy, or buddies, too. This is someone who you can go to the library with and sit with, and who will remind you to stay on task, wake you up from your fifteen minute power naps and take breaks with you. The goal here is to help motivate you to study and to take a break together as a fun reward. Again, this is designed to be a reciprocal agreement, and another positive consequence of this is that if you are encouraging your buddy to stay focused and get their work done, it reminds you to focus on your own work too.

However, if your buddy ends up distracting you and preventing you from getting your work done (even if they are good fun!) they are not a very good study buddy. Perhaps consider speaking to this buddy honestly and saying that you are finding them fun but, unfortunately, distracting. If the distraction continues perhaps you should use this friend for breaks, and social fun instead of as a study buddy.

Take advantage of the study resources available

Universities will have a number of resources available to help you manage your time and learn to study effectively. Check with student services for courses or options that they have to help you organize yourself – it might be workshops, mentoring or online resources – and a bonus is that they are free and designed especially for students. Please note that this book is not a 'how to study' guide, so if you are not sure precisely how best to study (as many students don't really know), look at the workshops or resources that the university might offer on this. You might ask your friends how they study – everyone will have their own system. Some people prefer scribbling notes, while others like mind maps. Some like to use audio recordings and mnemonics, others prefer a group study approach. It is probably best to try different ways and work out what is best for you.

The way you study will also likely involve a combination of styles, and will also depend on your course requirements. If you are learning languages, a good portion of your time will be spent on vocal learning, whereas if you are studying law, you will need to hit the books and read a lot of case law and precedents.

Finally, try to attend optional tutorials where they are offered. Often courses have additional tutorials that you can attend, which are really useful and give you good opportunity to clarify any work that you are not clear on.

Learn to say 'no'

It is really exciting starting university – so many new friends to meet, so many new experiences, so many social events and leisure activities. University offers a lot of clubs and societies where you can try new things or find people who are like-minded and share your interests. There will also be sports activities and gyms, and a lot of opportunities to be part of committees that help manage clubs or events. Or you might want to help organize social activities at your halls of residence or dorm, or start a new club. Perhaps you are also that person who gets FOMO and wants to be part of everything. Or you find it hard to turn down any requests for your help... Well, you get it – there are a lot of ways you could be kept busy and occupied.

But therein lies the problem. Overcommitting yourself means that there is less time for the thing you are there for – to study and pass your university course. This is not to say that you shouldn't make time for these things, but you need to keep them in balance so they don't interfere with your main reason for being at university.

If you are feeling under time pressure, know that it is OK to say 'no' to things. Saying 'no' to social events will not mean you'll never get asked again. Saying 'no' to a new experience is not something to mourn, as there will be plenty more new experiences at university and after you graduate. Saying 'no' to a request for help does not mean you don't care, or you are a terrible person, it just means that you have to prioritize your own needs for once.

If you look back to your weekly plan, you will hopefully still have a lot of fun things booked in, such as exercise, social time and study breaks. Saying 'no' to a few things will not prevent you from having fun or taking much needed breaks, it just means you have to look after your own study needs and prioritize your time. It will also mean you will really enjoy the non-study events that you have also made sure are in your timetable.

Summary

- There are some common problems students face regarding managing themselves and their time.
- Change your outlook to help you address negative patterns of thinking.
- Organize your notes, materials and workspace.
- Have a 'study buddy'.
- Treat your time at university like a job.
- Investigate what resources your university has on offer to help with study skills.
- Practise saying 'no' to things.

CHAPTER 7

WELLBEING

While you are at university, you also need to take into account your own wellbeing. Wellbeing refers to your mental and physical health, and is about finding ways to look after yourself, being resilient under pressure, and knowing what to do you if you are not feeling mentally or physically well.

There will be plenty of stressful times while you are at university including deadlines, exams, interviews for graduate school and so on. There are also a lot of stressful events that happen personally – as life goes on alongside university. There could be physical health or mental health issues, family issues, relationship or friend issues, financial stress, accommodation problems, work- or children-related problems, the list goes on. So, among the other demands on your time, it is important to ensure that you look after your wellbeing so you are strong enough to weather these stressors. This doesn't mean that these things won't affect you, but it will help you be more resilient and cope with them better.

This chapter covers some important ways to look after yourself while you are at university including tips to help you organize yourself to add them into your busy schedule, and they hold true for life after university as well. Some you may already know, but having a refresher is a good way to motivate yourself to make some positive changes in your lifestyle to support your wellbeing.

Sleep

This is a very important factor in maintaining your wellbeing. There are plenty of studies showing that we need good-quality sleep in order to stay healthy, and it turns out that most of us are not getting enough shut-eye. It can be difficult to get enough sleep – there's always study, work and socializing to be done, not to mention the fact of being continuously connected to a form of media, on a phone or streaming TV or movies. It all takes a severe toll on our sleep.

We need sleep in order to study and learn. It helps the cognitive functions that we need for study – paying attention, taking in information and processing it properly. Sleep helps us 'consolidate' the information we have learned during the day and file it away in the appropriate place, so we can recall it later.

Good quality sleep is generally accepted as:

- Sleeping most of the time while in bed (at least 85% of the total time you are in bed).
- Falling asleep in thirty minutes or less when you go to bed.
- Waking up no more than once per night.
- Being awake for twenty minutes or less during the night after initially falling asleep[i]. Although night waking is normal, and everyone wakes up as part of a standard sleep cycle, night awakenings become a problem when you fully wake up and cannot get back to sleep quickly.

In order to help you have a good sleep, putting in place some simple sleep hygiene practises can help.

Tips for better sleeping

- Try to maintain a consistent sleep schedule with the same bedtime and wake-up time every day. This helps to regulate your body's internal clock.

- Practise a relaxing bedtime routine, such as having a warm shower or bath, as this increases your body temperature and helps you prepare for sleep. Listening to peaceful music and dimming the lights can also help prepare your body for bed.
- Avoid napping during the day.
- Exercise daily (see p54).
- Try to ensure your sleep environment is not too hot or cold and that it is free from a lot of noise and light.
- Use bright light in the morning and during the day to help manage your body clock. Avoid bright light in the evening.
- Avoid alcohol, cigarettes and heavy meals in the evening. Although students do like to socialize at night, and this can include alcohol, make sure that this isn't on successive nights, and that you moderate your alcohol intake.
- Wind down at night after study – your body needs time to shift into sleep mode, so avoid electronics in the last hour before bed and do something relaxing like reading, playing or listening to music, or gentle stretching instead.
- If, after going to bed, you still can't sleep, get up and do something relaxing until you feel tired, then try going back to bed. The worst thing to do is lie in bed thinking 'I wish I could sleep', and getting yourself wound up, which will not help you get back to sleep.

Your circadian rhythm

The circadian rhythm is a 24-hour internal clock running in the background of your brain, which cycles between sleepiness and alertness at regular intervals. It regulates when you feel tired and lack energy, and when you feel alert and energized. For most people, the biggest dip in energy happens in the middle of the night (somewhere between 2 a.m. and 4 a.m., when they're usually fast asleep) and just after lunchtime (around 1 p.m. to 3 p.m., when you tend to crave a post-lunch nap). But if you are naturally a 'morning' or a 'night' person – a self-identified 'early bird' or 'night owl' – these times might be a bit different.

A part of your brain called the hypothalamus controls your circadian rhythm, and external factors such as light and darkness also impact on this internal clock. If it is dark, your eyes send a signal to the hypothalamus that it's time to feel tired. Your brain, in turn, sends a signal to your body to release melatonin, which makes your body tired and makes you want to go to sleep. That's why your internal circadian rhythm tends to coincide with the external cycle of daytime and night time – and it's also why the rise in use of backlit screens in bed is problematic for sleep as it disrupts your natural sleep/wake cycle by telling your brain it might be daytime!

The best time to study

In knowing how to best organize yourself and your time, it is important to know how and when you do your best work. You might already know this – you might be a morning person who works best in quiet soothing environments, or you might be someone who prefers studying at night and being in a busy library. However you work best, you need to harness that time and use it properly.

If you are morning person:

- Get up and do some study or coursework before breakfast.
- Go for a morning run or do some early morning exercise.
- Get up and go to the library for when it opens so you can get an hour or two of work done before it gets busy.
- Use this morning time for your most challenging work such as study, or writing a paper, or reading through research papers.

- Don't use this morning time for mindless tasks such as checking your emails or tabbing your notes or cleaning your room. Do this in the evening when you feel tired and can't focus as well on cognitively challenging tasks.

If you are an evening person:

- Use the afternoon and evening hours to do your more challenging work.
- Exercise around mid-morning or lunchtime, or late afternoon.
- If you find it hard to get going in the morning, use this time for less demanding tasks like checking emails and organizing your study notes.
- Even if you are an evening person, still keep a regular bedtime. Don't be fooled by the fact you are an evening person to let yourself stay up very late, and sleep-in in the morning. Lectures still take place early in the morning, whether you are a morning person or not!

And if you identify neither as a morning or evening person, well that's just fine – you probably have a very normal and regular internal clock and might be able to get up early and complete tasks or study later at night. You are lucky in that you can have the best of both worlds. You still might find there are times of the day when you work better than others and feel more energized, so harness this time and use it for your more cognitively demanding tasks, and when you are tired, do the easier tasks such as organizing your notes, cleaning your room or finding research papers in the library.

If your sleep has been disturbed or you have been 'burning the candle at both ends', you will notice that you don't feel as energized and alert at times that you think you should. Jet lag is a good example of your circadian rhythm being out of sync! Feeling tired and hungry at unusual times of the day, being alert during the night, finding it hard to fall asleep are all signs of a disrupted sleep cycle. And be aware that taking long naps during the day is not going to help. They can perpetuate a disrupted sleep cycle and result in you going to bed even later and sleeping later in the mornings, which can lead to a vicious cycle of unhealthy sleep habits. The good news is that you can get your circadian rhythm back into step after a few days by observing day/night hours, and regular sleeping and eating patterns.

A quick note about power naps. Unlike longer naps, these have had some good feedback. They are short naps of, say, fifteen to twenty minutes that might help you take a break and have a quick recharge. You may need to set an alarm, however, and need to have the self-discipline to make sure you get back to work straight after!

Finally, poor sleeping can also be part of a medical issue or a mental health problem such as depression or anxiety. If you continue to have trouble sleeping, please see your doctor to discuss this and explore options to help you sleep better. This might be medication or is increasingly likely to be a psychological treatment focused on sleep.

Exercise

You will no doubt know about the positive results exercise has been shown to have on both your physical and your mental health. Exercise is beneficial for many health reasons, including being important for your brain. It is associated with improvements in memory, concentration and attention – all vital cognitive processes for study and coursework. One recent study found that regular aerobic exercise seems to increase the size of the hippocampus, the brain area involved in verbal memory and learning. Exercise reduces insulin resistance and inflammation, and stimulates the release of growth factors – chemicals in the brain that affect the health of brain cells, the growth of new blood vessels in the brain, and even the abundance and survival of new brain cells.

So, exercise actually repairs our brain and grows it, which is pretty amazing! Exercise also improves mood and sleep, and reduces stress and anxiety – so it's an all-round winner.

The take-home message here is DO SOME EXERCISE. It is recommended that adults take about thirty minutes of moderate exercise a day – this could be walking quickly to lectures or to the supermarket, playing a team sport, cycling, walking with friends, going hiking, and so on. It doesn't have to be training for a marathon or competing at the Olympics. You can easily build it into your day. If anyone says, 'I don't have time for exercise', I would strongly disagree – the minimum recommended amount of exercise is three and a half hours out of a whopping 168 hours a week – roughly 2% of your time (or around 3% of your waking hours, generously accounting for eight hours of sleep a night!).

Exercise helps with study and is good stress relief. You can build it in to suit your lifestyle and it can be a fun, social thing – so, perhaps try a new team sport or jog around the park with a friend. Universities often have a student gym that offers subsidized fees, and there are plenty of online options for free exercise classes and yoga. You can always find something that suits your schedule and budget.

Eating well

As with exercise, there is a lot of information available on healthy eating and the importance of a balanced diet for longevity of life, physical wellbeing and good mental health. There is some fascinating recent research linking good mental health with the types of food you eat and how they interact in your gut with bacteria and microbes[ii]. It would be hard to list all the research findings and recommendations, so here is a brief summary of general healthy eating advice:

- Eat lots of fruit and vegetables
- Eat unprocessed foods

- Cut down on sugar and salt (they hide in a lot of processed foods!)
- Eat lots of fibrous food including legumes and wholemeal grains
- Moderate alcohol and caffeine consumption
- Eat a wide variety of foods
- If you eat meat, try to restrict this to a couple of times a week

Rigid dieting or highly restrictive eating, such as cutting out all chocolate, is unhelpful because people on such diets seldom maintain the weight they lost once they stop the dieting. Also, cutting out entire food groups often leads to an unhelpful cycle of bingeing and restricting. Balance, variety and moderation are key.

Being a student often means that you are both time poor and cash poor so going for a leisurely trip to the supermarket to buy only organic produce might not be realistic. But you don't need a lot of money, or even a lot of spare time, to eat properly.

Tips for healthy eating on a budget for a busy student

- Spend some time planning out meals and to a budget – this means only one trip to the supermarket a week. And book this time into your weekly timetable.
- Plan your shopping trip for a time when the supermarkets are offering discounted food (they usually do this at the end of each day for products that are expiring but are still fine to eat).
- If you live in a shared house you could have a cooking roster so you might only cook once or twice a week. This will also help to share the cost of food.

- If you live on your own, or prefer to cook on your own, experiment with batch cooking whereby you cook one big batch of meals a week and freeze individual portions. Again, make time for this in your weekly schedule.
- A lot of cheaper groceries, such as beans, pulses and some fish, are also available canned and this can be very cost effective. Also, frozen vegetables have been shown to be as nutritionally good to the fresh ones available and are also much cheaper to buy.
- Invest in a good hot drink flask – this will allow you to make your own hot drinks to take with you for your day at university, which can save money (and the planet).
- Learn a couple of easy 'go to' nutritious and filling recipes that you can always call on, and can repeat and alter slightly so you don't get bored.
- Cook enough the night before to provide for lunch the next day – this means you will have a healthy lunch and won't spend a lot of money on overpriced (and not necessarily nutritious) sandwiches.

And if you believe that your diet is causing you problems, such as digestive issues, sore guts, constipation, bloating, etc., make an appointment with your doctor to discuss this. These things can often be easily resolved but are always worth getting checked out, as digestion and gut problems can be painful at times and leave you feeling tired, lethargic and anxious, which can have a detrimental effect on your studying.

Socializing and connection

University offers amazing social opportunities. Human beings thrive on social connection and positive interactions with each other, and there is a confirmed link between reported levels of happiness and positive social relationships[iii]. We like to feel that we belong, and to interact with other people, but sometimes it can be hard to do. This might be because you are naturally introverted, socially anxious, have mental health or physical health problems that make it hard to go out to social events, or maybe have had bad experiences in relationships (being bullied or rejected) in the past. Even in busy dorms and flats, or with busy class timetables, it can be hard to make time to socialize, but it is important for your wellbeing and happiness that you make the effort. University offers a great opportunity to meet like-minded people who have similar interests and hobbies to you. There are lots of clubs and social events on offer, so be sure to try some. To socialize and meet some new people you could:

- Join a club that you are interested in.
- Try something new. Never tried rock climbing? Find a beginners or taster class.
- Volunteer at a charity.
- Go to a regular exercise class, such as yoga or Zumba.
- Volunteer to help at an event, such as a sports or theatre event.
- Turn up to social events organized at your dormitory or hall.
- Join some online forums and write a blog.

Looking after your health and learning

It is worth acknowledging that many students come to university with pre-existing mental health conditions, physical health needs or other issues that impact their learning. Examples of these might include ADHD, dyslexia, depression, diabetes, migraines and more. These could be recent issues or longer-term problems, and if you fall into this category you might have a good handle on your issues or you might require some ongoing monitoring and support. It is important to keep on top of any such needs, so make sure that you find out what support is available for you at your university and book in any appointments in advance.

General health checklist

- Investigate what kind of resources the university offers – they should have counseling services for mental health support, disability services for students with a disability, and medical services for students with medical and psychological conditions.
- Check with disability services if they can offer you extra support. They might be able to arrange for you to have extra time in exams, for example, or be able to provide you with study resources or extra tutorials.
- Check where the student counseling services are located and book in an appointment when you arrive.
- Make sure you arrange a new doctor close to university and bring with you any notes or medical history you need.
- Arrange for any medications to be on repeat to save time and hassle (some medications will not be able to be prescribed on repeat so you will need to check with your doctor).
- And finally, book in any appointments you need in that semester or term in advance as far as is

possible. You don't want to get to the final week and really need to see your doctor for medication but find there are no appointments left – this will cause you more stress that you can avoid with some planning.

Summary

- Looking after your wellbeing at university is important to keep you mentally and physically healthy.
- Sleep, eating well and exercise are key for keeping healthy, feeling energized and for the cognitive demands of study.
- Social connection is important to feel happy and there are many different opportunities to socialize when you are at university.
- If you have problems with your sleep or diet, seek help from you doctor. Such problems can have a significant impact on your wellbeing but might be easily resolved.
- Find out what support is available for any mental health, medical or disability needs you may have.
- Make sure you make any appointments you need in advance where you can, and get your prescriptions on repeat where possible.

CHAPTER 8

ANXIETY, PERFECTIONISM AND PROCRASTINATION

I have worked for many years as a clinical psychologist and during this time I have encountered many students who have psychological problems that make it difficult to manage themselves at university. The three main culprits are anxiety, procrastination and perfectionism, and they are usually interlinked. For example, students might feel anxious due to their procrastination; they might be procrastinating because they are perfectionists; they might feel anxious due to perfectionism or they might have a standalone anxiety problem that causes problems in other ways.

Anxiety

Anxiety is a very human condition. It is an interplay of your thoughts, emotions, physiology and behavioral responses. Everyone experiences anxiety to some degree and it is a normal reaction to something you perceive as a threat. For example, if you believe you are being followed on your way home at night, you are likely to react both emotionally and physiologically. Your emotional reaction may be one of fear. Physiologically, you may start to sweat and shake and feel your heart rate increase. Your cognitive response is to think you are in danger. No matter that the person could just walk past and pay you no attention; you have responded instinctively to what you perceive as a threat.

A normal human reaction to perceived threat

Anxiety has a pretty impressive physiological reaction known as the 'fight, flight or freeze' response. Your body releases the neurochemicals cortisol and adrenaline, which are hormones that play an important role in this response. More cortisol in your system gives you quick bursts of energy for survival and lower sensitivity to pain, and it curbs functions that are nonessential – it suppresses your digestive system, for example. Adrenaline makes your heart beat faster and your lungs breathe more efficiently, and it sends more blood to the brain and muscles, which increases your blood pressure, makes you more alert and gives you energy to either fight or flee.

Fight, flight or freeze is an evolutionary response from prehistoric times that has usefully stayed with us. It is an innate, protective response to keep us safe. Of course, this response makes more sense when the threat is obvious, such as a sabre-toothed tiger running towards our ancestors. However, as we have developed as humans and become more sophisticated and complex in the way we live, it is often harder now to identify what a 'threat' really is. Today, threats are not just physical; they can be mental and emotional, too. So, while our threat system still operates as it did with our ancestors, it can be much trickier for us to pin down the actual threat, which means our threat system misfires and we can end up with anxiety problems.

For example, the threat of failing your course at university could cause you as much anxiety, relatively speaking, as the sabre-toothed tiger did to our cavemen ancestors. Although this threat doesn't mean you will die, there is the threat of debt, losing your place on the course, loss of status, not being able to get a place on a graduate programme, embarrassment – and of these things are all threats to your survival in today's world.

Physical symptoms of anxiety can include:

- Increased heart rate
- Startle response
- Sweating
- Feeling hot/panicky
- Dry mouth
- Nausea or upset stomach
- Tense muscles
- Narrowed vision (tunnel vision)

You could experience some of these physical symptoms while watching a scary movie or during an exam, or perhaps even sitting in a lecture thinking about your finals or the amount of coursework you have on your plate. I would be surprised if you cannot recall a single time when you experienced the physiological changes of anxiety in your body. Because, as I repeat, **anxiety is a normal human condition and we all experience it**, even the most outwardly calm students. However, even though anxiety is normal, if it is misplaced or misdirected it can become a problem and you might find yourself experiencing it too frequently and/or intensely. The words 'stress', 'worry', 'fear', 'panic', 'keyed up' and 'on edge' are used in relation to everyday occurrences but these terms – and many others – all refer to anxiety.

Consequences of anxiety at university

Anxiety can cause problems in a lot of ways for students and can directly affect your ability to study and complete your coursework. It can cause:

- Avoidance of coursework
- Avoidance of lectures and tutorials
- Difficulty studying or taking in information (have your ever tried to focus on something whilst feeling overwhelmed with anxiety?)
- Problems taking exams
- Problems with motivation and attendance
- Difficulties starting coursework
- Delays in handing in work
- Problems sleeping
- Unhappiness and depression
- Avoidance of people or social events
- Low self-esteem
- Panic attacks
- Constant worry

The term 'anxiety' covers the full range of anxiety presentations and symptoms, from minor symptoms – such as being worried that you will be late handing in a paper – to severe anxiety, which manifests itself in an actual diagnosable disorder such as panic disorder, general anxiety disorder, social anxiety or OCD. When you have anxiety that is interfering significantly in your studies, personal or social life, it is very possible that you have an anxiety disorder. If you think this might be the case for you, you need to speak to your doctor straight away and get some treatment for it so it doesn't continue to interfere with your studies and your enjoyment at university. You can also check in with student counseling services as they may offer some help for anxiety, which may be all you need if you are suffering from a milder form.

Perfectionism

Clinical perfectionism is when people strive for perfection in what they do at a detrimental cost. We call it 'clinical' perfectionism when it means it is at a level that causes significant impairment in someone's ability to function.

It is often seen in university students and can become problematic if it is left unchecked.

Perfectionism is defined as 'setting excessively high and unrealistic standards for yourself, and measuring your self-worth only in achievements'. That means you set very high standards that you hold yourself to, and when you don't achieve them, which you often won't because they are unrealistic, you become very self-critical and can feel depressed and anxious.

This is not the same as simply having high standards. You may hold yourself to high standards in your behavior and performance, and this is fine, as long as there is some flexibility in this. For example, you may set yourself the goal for an A average, and if you receive a B on one paper you might be disappointed initially, but you don't internalize this as a failure and allow it to stop you from moving on with your studies and having fun. Whereas if you suffer from clinical perfectionism, you might find it hard to stop thinking about this B, believe it represents a failure and believe you now have to spend all your spare time studying to make sure it doesn't happen again.

There are a lot of downsides to clinical perfectionism. It is linked to emotional problems and other responses that impact on being able to be organized and successfully complete your academic commitments. These can include:

- Procrastination because you are worried that whatever you do won't be good enough, so it makes it difficult to start.
- Spending excessively long on coursework because it needs to be 'perfect'.
- Feeling anxious and overwhelmed as a result of the pressure you put on yourself.
- Being very self-critical and hard on yourself.
- Not allowing yourself to have a 'break' or 'downtime' because you believe it is lazy.

- Being perfectionistic about other areas in your life including appearance, diet, exercise, relationships, which causes problems in a similar way.
- Never believing your work is 'good enough' or you have done enough.
- Feeling shame, embarrassment and feeling low or depressed.
- Being very worried about how other people think about you.
- You might think you don't have a problem and that there is nothing wrong with having extremely high standards.
- You worry about failing.
- You constantly compare yourself to others.
- You spend an excessive amount of time on things that will not directly benefit your study or coursework, such as organizing your materials, rewriting or typing your notes.
- You pay excessive attention to detail, such as rewriting emails multiple times until they sound just right.
- You feel keyed up and on edge a lot.
- You find you need a 'release' in self-harming, alcohol or drug use.

Perfectionism is also linked to a number of mental health disorders, including:

- Depression and anxiety
- Obsessive Compulsive Disorder (OCD)
- Body Dysmorphic Disorder (BDD)
- Social Anxiety
- Generalized Anxiety Disorder
- Eating disorders (anorexia, bulimia and binge eating)
- Thoughts of suicide
- Addiction problems
- Self-harming

Joan's Story

Joan was in her first year at medical school. She had always set high standards for herself, and if she didn't get top marks in any test or assignment, she became depressed and beat herself up. She spent all her evenings studying, and never went to social events or allowed herself to have fun. Whenever she didn't get an A or A+ she blamed herself for being lazy and not trying hard enough, and she began to self-harm as a way to cope with the pressure she put on herself. Joan wasn't enjoying university and was feeling very down, and worried she had made the wrong choice in studying medicine. Eventually, her unhappiness led Joan to make an appointment with a university doctor to discuss her worries and to get some guidance on how to start feeling better about herself and being at university.

If you think you have some of these traits and this is negatively impacting on your time at university, and you are finding it difficult to keep on top of your coursework, you need to speak to someone about this. Make an appointment with your doctor, or a university counselor. There is good help available and you don't have to let perfectionism ruin your time at university. Plus, if you don't try to change these things now, you will likely still have problems with perfectionism when you leave university and start in the job market, and you will still suffer from the negative aspects of perfectionism.

Procrastination

Ever thought, 'there's not enough time!', or panicked when a due date for a report or an assignment loomed? Have you ever felt anxious or overwhelmed because you had too many commitments, or avoided getting started on a project because you didn't know where to start? Academic procrastination is when you leave academic tasks, such as preparing for exams and doing coursework, to the last minute and feel anxious because of this.

There are two types of procrastinators–passive procrastinators and active procrastinators. Passive procrastination is what we typically think of as procrastination: getting distracted and delaying starting a task. Active procrastination describes those people who work better under pressure – they prefer the adrenaline rush and intense focus that comes with a deadline and might choose to start tasks later in order to achieve this.

If you are passive procrastinator, then it might well have a negative effect on your grades, whereas those who like the adrenaline and working under pressure at the last minute are less likely to see their grades affected. If doing things late and not leaving enough time for tasks or study is causing you distress, then you are most likely a passive procrastinator. Whereas if you enjoy, and perhaps even look forward to the challenge of trying to complete tasks late, then you are probably an active procrastinator.

Procrastination can happen for many reasons, but some of the main causes are:

- The fear of making mistakes (perfectionism)
- Feeling too overwhelmed and not knowing where to start
- Postponing tasks that require attention
- Poor time management
- Difficulty making decisions
- Lacking confidence in your own ability to complete the task

Joan's Story

Joan had a paper due at the end of the following week. She had been putting off starting work as she felt she didn't understand it properly and had wanted to speak to her professor before deciding on a topic. Joan had a history of leaving things until the last minute and feeling really stressed, staying up all night trying to finish work and often being late handing it in (which resulted in a grade penalty). Joan became sick of feeling so stressed out so she decided to seek help from the student wellbeing services and made an appointment to speak with a counselor. This helped her identify her problem and work on some solutions.

There are some simple ways to beat your procrastination if it is a problem for you, too.

Break each job down into the smallest and simplest tasks

If you are feeling overwhelmed and unsure where to start, the best thing to do is break the task down into the smallest step to start. Don't know where to start on your paper? Write the title, your name and the first opening sentence. Done! Don't know where to start in studying? Open the book to lesson one and read the first paragraph. Done! These are just small steps, but they will open the door for you and, step-by-step, you will get closer to your end goal.

You can also set yourself a time limit. Instead of thinking, I need to study all week nonstop, you can set yourself a target of thirty minutes and then take a break. This is much more manageable and, who knows, you might even feel like continuing with study.

Worried you will make a mistake

Your procrastination here is likely tied to perfectionism, as discussed above. You will need to tackle your perfectionism as well, but know that your performance in these tasks are not an evaluation on you as a person. You will need to work on separating your self-worth from tasks and try to see them for what they are – just a task. Your worth as a person is not defined by one academic essay or grade. You are worth much, much more than that.

Difficulty making decisions

If you have a problem making decisions, it is probably from worry that you will make the wrong decision or a belief that there is a perfect decision. A decision cannot be right or wrong, or perfect. It is the outcome that determines whether or not you made the right decision. So, in that moment, there is no right or wrong, just a decision to be made. Put a timer on the decision you are trying to make – one minute. Then go with that decision, and it doesn't matter if it doesn't 'feel' right – just go with it. A decision is made and soon it won't bother you any more – the 'doesn't feel right' feeling doesn't last forever.

Remind yourself of the bigger picture

It can be easy to get caught up in other, more fun tasks, with every intention of studying later, and writing that paper due in a few weeks. But you need to remind yourself that you are at university to get your degree, and that you can have fun around that task, but not at the expense of it.

Remind yourself of all your achievements to date

If you lack confidence in your ability to do the task, just pause and remind yourself of where you are – you made it to university and have successfully completed many hurdles on your way to get there. You would not be there if you didn't have the skillset or drive to make it. You can do this, and you will.

Improve your time management

Well that's what we have covered in a lot of this book! It is within your control and you can learn the skills you need to successfully manage your time at university

Summary

- Three common problems can impact on your self-organization: anxiety, perfectionism and procrastination.
- These problems are often interlinked, and it is likely if you have one of these problems that you will also be affected by the others.
- Anxiety is normal and gives rise to the fight, flight or freeze response. However, if you experience anxiety too much it can be a problem and might impact negatively on your time at university.
- Perfectionism is having extremely high standards and being very self-critical, and can lead to a lot of mental health problems as well as difficulties completing coursework.
- Procrastination is when you delay tasks to your detriment. There are some practical solutions that can help you overcome procrastination.
- If your anxiety or perfectionism is impacting your time at university, you should speak to your doctor to get some help. They can also refer you to a psychologist or counselors who are trained to help in these areas.
- If procrastination is part of an anxiety problem or perfectionism, you will need to get help with these problems in order to tackle the procrastination.

CHAPTER 9

FINAL WORDS

University is an exciting and special time in your life. You are finding your way through the first steps of being completely independent for your living and learning, developing lifelong friendships, having amazing learning and social experiences, being exposed to new philosophies and ideas, and thinking about the early steps in your future career. But you need to organize yourself to make the most of these opportunities.

Hopefully, this book has shown you that with some planning you can be organized so that you use your time at university most effectively and give yourself the best chance to meet your academic goals while looking after your health and wellbeing at the same time. Not only will some planning and thinking ahead make you more likely to achieve well academically, it will also make you less stressed and more primed to enjoy your time at university.

There is no single system that works for everybody. How you work and when you work will depend on your how demanding your coursework is, other commitments, personal circumstances, and accessibility. Focus on developing a system that works for you. If things are not working, review it! Spend some time thinking about what is going wrong and why and then make a plan to change it. It may be that the system you used is no longer working for various reasons and you need to change it. All it might take is a slight tweak, or perhaps an overhaul in your working patterns, but it is better to review and update it so you can make the most of your time at university.

Learning how to organize yourself is also an excellent blueprint for life. After university, life continues to be busy and other demands will take up your time – but if you have the basic skills of self-management and knowing how to organize your time effectively, you can continue to make the most out of life and be a successful person.

Good luck for your time at university. Be organized, and you will succeed.

REFERENCES

Ariga, A. & Lieras, A. (2011). Brief and rare mental "breaks" keep you focused: Deactivation and reactivation of task goals preempt vigilance decrements. *Cognition*. 118, 439–43.

Baumeister, R. F. & Leary, M. R. (1995). The Need to Belong: Desire for Interpersonal Attachments as a Fundamental Human Motivation. *Psychology Bulletin*. 117(3): 497–529.

Çapan, B. E. (2010). Relationship among perfectionism, academic procrastination and life satisfaction of university students. *Procedia-Social and Behavioral Sciences*. 5, 1665–71.

Hepburn, C., Ortiz, V. & Locksley, A. (1984). Morning and evening people: Examination of an identifying scale and of social-and self-perceptions of personality differences. *Journal of Research in Personality*. 18(1), 99–109.

Kim, S., Fernandez, S. & Terrier, L. (2017). Procrastination, personality traits, and academic performance: When active and passive procrastination tell a different story. *Personality and Individual Differences*. 108, 154–57.

Komarraju, M., Karau, S. J., Schmeck, R. R. & Avdic, A. (2011). The Big Five personality traits, learning styles, and academic achievement. *Personality and individual differences*. 51(4), 472–77.

Milgram, N., Marshevsky, S. & Sadeh, C. (1995). Correlates of academic procrastination: Discomfort, task aversiveness, and task capability. *The Journal of Psychology*. 129, 145–55.

Milgram, N., Mey-Tal, G. & Levison, Y. (1998). Procrastination, generalized or specific, in college students and their parents. *Personality and Individual Differences.* 25, 297–316.

Mosely, M. (2017). *Clever Guts Diet.* London: Short Books Ltd.

Ohayon, M. et al. (2017). National Sleep Foundation's Sleep Quality Recommendations: First Report. *Sleep Health.* 3(1): 6.

Preckel, F., Lipnevich, A. A., Schneider, S. & Roberts, R. D. (2011). Chronotype, cognitive abilities, and academic achievement: A meta-analytic investigation. *Learning and Individual Differences.* 21, 483–92.

Saddler, C. D. & Sacks, L. A. (1993). Multidimensional Perfectionism and Academic Procrastination: Relationships with Depression in University Students. *Psychological reports.* 73(3 part 1), 863–71.

Sansgiry, S. S., Bhosle, M. & Sail, K. (2006). Factors that affect academic performance among pharmacy students. *American journal of pharmaceutical education.* 70(5).

Schouwenburg, H. & Lay, C. H. (1995). Trait procrastination and the big five factors of personality. *Personality and Individual Differences.* 18, 481–90.

Schouwenburg, H. C. (1992). Procrastinators and fear of failure: An exploration of reasons for procrastination. *European Journal of Personality.* 6, 225–36.

Senecal, C., Koestner, R. & Vallerand, R. J. (1995). Self-regulation and academic procrastination. *The Journal of Social Psychology.* 135, 607–19.

Solomon, L. J. & Rothblum, E. D. (1984). Academic procrastination: frequency and cognitive-behavioral correlates. *Journal of Counseling Psychology.* 31, 503–09.

Vanderkam, L. (2010). 168 hours: You have more time than you think. New York, NY: Penguin.

TriggerHub.org is one of the most elite and scientifically proven forms of mental health intervention

Trigger Publishing is the leading independent mental health and wellbeing publisher in the UK and US. Clinical and scientific research conducted by assistant professor Dr Kristin Kosyluk and her highly acclaimed team in the Department of Mental Health Law & Policy at the University of South Florida (USF), as well as complementary research by her peers across the US, has independently verified the power of lived experience as a core component in achieving mental health prosperity. Specifically, the lived experiences contained within our bibliotherapeutic books are intrinsic elements in reducing stigma, making those with poor mental health feel less alone, providing the privacy they need to heal, ensuring they know the essential steps to kick-start their own journeys to recovery, and providing hope and inspiration when they need it most.

Delivered through TriggerHub, our unique online portal and accompanying smartphone app, we make our library of bibliotherapeutic titles and other vital resources accessible to individuals and organizations anywhere, at any time and with complete privacy, a crucial element of recovery. As such, TriggerHub is the primary recommendation across the UK and US for the delivery of lived experiences.

At Trigger Publishing and TriggerHub, we proudly lead the way in making the unseen become seen. We are dedicated to humanizing mental health, breaking stigma and challenging outdated societal values to create real action and impact. Find out more about our world-leading work with lived experience and bibliotherapy via triggerhub.org, or by joining us on:

🐦 @triggerhub_

 @triggerhub.org

 @triggerhub_

Printed in the USA
CPSIA information can be obtained
at www.ICGtesting.com
JSHW032113280624
65591JS00007B/57

9 781837 963775